LANCASHIRE'S RAILWAYS: 1978 – PRESENT

MARTYN HILBERT

AMBERLEY

First published 2024

Amberley Publishing
The Hill, Stroud
Gloucestershire, GL5 4EP

www.amberley-books.com

Copyright © Martyn Hilbert, 2024

The right of Martyn Hilbert to be identified as
the Author of this work has been asserted in
accordance with the Copyrights, Designs and
Patents Act 1988.

ISBN 978 1 3981 1471 5 (print)
ISBN 978 1 3981 1472 2 (ebook)

British Library Cataloguing in Publication Data.
A catalogue record for this book is available from
the British Library.

Origination by Amberley Publishing.
Printed in the UK.

Introduction

Welcome to Lancashire – the 'Red Rose County'. Lancashire is a large, diverse and contrasting part of north-west England. The county currently has a total area of 1,189 square miles (3,080 square kilometres) and is home to 1,449,300 people. It has borders with Cumbria, North and West Yorkshire, Greater Manchester and Merseyside. The present geographical encompassment of Lancashire is the result of the Local Government Act of 1972; before this, the cities of Liverpool and Manchester were a part of the 'Red Rose County'. Geographically, the county has the Pennines running north–south along its eastern fringe, with the Lakeland fells to the north. North Lancashire runs westward to the seaside resort of Morecambe and the port of Heysham, whilst south of the River Lune and the city of Lancaster a pastoral landscape runs towards the Fylde coast, home to the former fishing port of Fleetwood and the seaside resorts of Blackpool and Lytham St Annes. Central Lancashire is dominated by Preston (a city since 2008) and is now the administrative capital of the county. East from Preston is the scenic Ribble Valley, with east Lancashire along its southern fringe. South from Preston are the towns of Chorley, Bolton and Wigan. West Lancashire, which is largely agricultural, runs to the south of the Ribble Estuary and encompasses the market town of Ormskirk and the seaside resort of Southport.

Lancashire played a leading role in the Industrial Revolution, with two commodities dominating the area: coal and cotton. At the height of the Lancashire coal industry in 1907, the numerous collieries across the area produced over 26 million tons of coal. In common with the rest of the UK's deep coal mining industry, the Lancashire Coalfield went into decline in the 1960s and 1970s. The last colliery to close was at Parkside, Newton-le-Willows, in 1993.

The cotton industry, in particular cotton spinning, reached its zenith at the turn of the nineteenth century. Lancashire had the largest cotton industry in the world. It was home to over 2,600 mills, which produced 50 per cent of all the world's cotton goods and provided employment for over 500,000 people. By 1900, the east Lancashire town of Burnley was known as the cotton-weaving capital of the world. The county was synonymous with its cotton towns: Accrington, Bacup, Blackburn, Bolton, Brierfield, Burnley, Bury, Chorley, Colne, Darwen, Haslingden, Nelson, Oldham, Oswaldtwistle, Padiham, Preston, Rawtenstall, Rochdale and Wigan. Their urban landscapes were dominated by spinning mills large and small, with tall chimneys and streets of terraced housing. The last large cotton spinning mill was opened at Bamber Bridge in 1907, but in the 1920s and 1930s the industry went into decline and after a brief renaissance after the Second World War, it sadly disappeared altogether.

From their earliest beginnings in the 1830s, the railways in Lancashire aided the expansion of industry, commerce, urban expansion and access to the coast and country. Without the railways, Lancashire would not have become the industrial powerhouse it did in the nineteenth and early twentieth centuries. Similarly, the seaside resorts of Blackpool, Morecambe and Southport would not have developed without the railways that took many thousands on day trips and holidays.

Up until the early 1960s the county had a complex and busy rail network that 'buzzed with activity'. Sadly, in common with other parts of the UK, industrial decline, the expansion of the road and motorway networks, the convenience of moving goods by road, the Beeching

Report and improving motor vehicle technology and its accessibility, all aided the reduction of the Lancashire railway network. Despite the contractions of the 1960s, all was not lost. The electrification of the West Coast Main Line (WCML) north of Weaver Junction, through Wigan, Preston and Lancaster to Carlisle and Glasgow Central, which was completed in 1974, brought about a transformation of Anglo-Scottish services that served Lancashire. As the road and motorway networks have become more congested, passenger numbers across the county have grown over the years. The much-needed electrification between Liverpool and Manchester and Liverpool to Wigan was completed in 2015, and electrification of the busy Manchester to Blackpool (via Bolton) corridor in 2019, along with the introduction of new Class 195/331 DMU/EMUs in 2020 and a major refurbishment of the Northern Class 150/156/158 DMU fleet, have all a refreshed the system and the places it serves.

In 2022, passenger services across Lancashire were provided by Avanti West Coast, Merseyrail, Northern and Transpennine Express. Freight is handled by Colas Rail, DB Cargo, DRS, Freightliner and GBRf. In an age where environmental issues are important, the railways of Lancashire still have their part to play.

The images in this book follow a north–south journey across the county. Some locations that were once inside Lancashire's boundaries but are now part of Cumbria, Greater Manchester and Merseyside are also included. Many of the main lines, secondary routes, branch lines, industrial lines, heritage railways, tramways and miniature railways are illustrated. The images selected are from the period 1978–2022 and are a mix of scanned colour transparencies and digital images. Hopefully they will give a flavour of the railways across Lancashire over the years. They may also be an inspiration to get out and about on the remaining Lancashire railway network to travel, record and enjoy the daily scene. One day it will all be history.

Thank you to the team at Amberley Publishing for their assistance; thanks to Matt Engh for the map; and, as always, thanks to my wife Gillian.

Martyn Hilbert
Preston, Lancashire

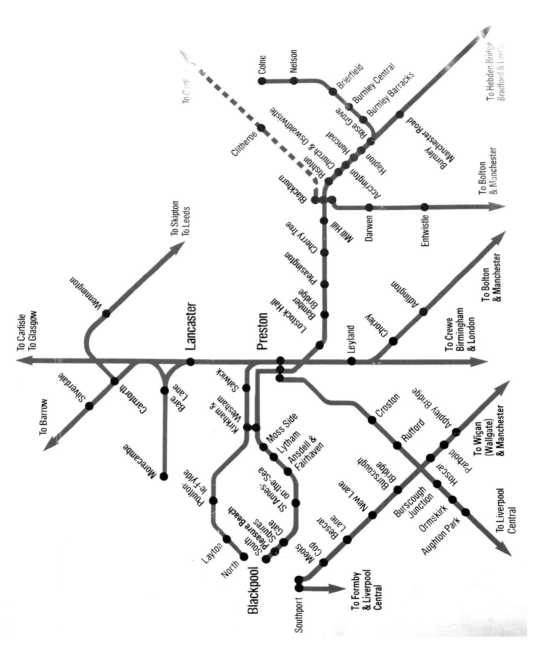

A schematic British Rail (BR) map of Lancashire routes from the 1980s.

In its BR Provincial Services Sprinter livery, Class 156 No. 156425 was awaiting departure from Grange-over-Sands with the 10.53 Barrow-in-Furness to Manchester Airport service on 31 May 1996. The station at Grange is located alongside Morecambe Bay, and has retained the Furness Railway buildings and platform canopies from 1864.

A pair of DRS Class 37/6s, Nos 37602 and 37603, were passing Arnside with the 08.49 Sellafield to Crewe nuclear flask working on 5 November 2016. The large nuclear processing plant at Sellafield on the Cumbrian coast has ensured the survival of the Furness line between Carnforth and Carlisle.

In First North Western livery with Northern branding, Class 153 single-unit No. 153330 was stood at Silverdale with the 14.10 Lancaster to Carlisle (via Barrow and Workington) on 20 August 1995. The 120-mile scenic journey along the Cumbrian coast was a good distance from the 153's home depot at Newton Heath, east Manchester.

On 19 April 2003, EWS-liveried Class 47 No. 47760 *Ribblehead Viaduct* was passing over Carnforth station junction with the return NENTA, the Cumbrian and Eskdale Explorer excursion from Ravenglass to Norwich. The coaching stock was a Norwich Crown Point Depot, Anglia Railways Mk 2 set normally used on services from London Liverpool Street to Norwich.

Northern Class 158 No. 158860 was awaiting departure from Wennington with the 12.18 Leeds to Morecambe service on 2 May 2022. Now a quiet country station on the north fringe of Lancashire, Wennington was once a busy junction. The now closed line once ran to Lancaster along the Lune Valley via Halton and Hornby.

Northern three-car Class 144 No. 144015 was passing Capernwray while working the 10.19 Leeds to Heysham (via Lancaster and Morecambe) service on 5 November 2016. The 'Little North Western' route from Settle Junction to Carnforth has a basic service every two hours in both directions.

Northern CAF-built Class 195/1 No. 195124 was arriving at Carnforth with the 14.50 Barrow-in-Furness to Manchester Airport service on 18 April 2022. Introduced in 2019, Northern has a fleet of thirty-three three-car Class 195/1 DMUs.

Lancashire & Yorkshire Railway Aspinall 0-6-0 No. 1300, with BR Mk 1 coaches *Beryl* (128) and *Eileen* (125) in tow, was heading along the 1-mile single-track demonstration line at Steamtown Carnforth on 29 August 1992. Based at the former Carnforth MPD, Steamtown closed as a visitor attraction in 1997 and is the now the headquarters of West Coast Railways.

With the LMS concrete-built coal and ash plants dating from 1944 dominating the skyline, withdrawn Class 31s Nos 31275 and 31410 were stored in the yard at Carnforth on 4 September 1999. No. 31410 eventually went into preservation and was based at Kirkby Stephen East, but was subsequently scrapped in 2014. No. 31275 was scrapped at Carnforth in 2005.

Class 86/2 No. 86226, on 17 April 1978, was passing Carnforth North Junction with a Crewe to Carlisle parcels/mail working that included a Mk 1 BSK coach in the formation.

Class 31 No. 31130 in Railfreight Coal Sector livery with barrier wagons and a brake van are stabled in the Down sidings at Carnforth on 10 May 1992. The train would be en route to BNFL Sellafield to collect nuclear flask wagons. These trains were amongst the last in the UK to use a brake van in the traditional manner.

With its pantograph stretched high, DRS Class 88 No. 88005 *Minerva* was about to pass over the level crossing at Hest Bank with the 14.43 Mossend Euroterminal to Daventry Tesco service on 27 August 2017. The BR Type 15 signal box that once controlled the barriers here was closed in May 2013, when operation passed to the Preston PSB via CCTV.

Transpennine Express Class 350/4 No. 350408 was passing Hest Bank with the 10.10 Manchester Airport to Edinburgh service on 23 February 2019. The unit is passing over the turnout for the bi-directional single line to Bare Lane on the Morecambe branch. Along the 401-mile WCML, it is at Hest Bank that the line is closest to the coast.

Rusty rails and derelict railway land were greeting Greater Manchester-liveried Class 142 No. 142013 as it arrived at Morecambe Promenade with the 12.03 from Lancaster on 6 November 1993. The seafront terminus was opened by the Midland Railway in 1907. The station was closed in February 1994 and a new one was built a few hundred yards away, enabling the original station site to be redeveloped.

The end of the line at Morecambe. Northern Class 142 No. 142058 was awaiting departure with the 14.22 to Lancaster 24 August 2019. Opened in 1994, the basic station at Morecambe has two platforms and a run-round loop.

The single-track branch from Morecambe to Heysham Port is just over 4 miles in length. While Heysham has vehicular passenger and freight ferry sailings to the Isle of Man and Northern Ireland, there is just one passenger service a day out and back from Lancaster, which reverses at Morecambe. On 6 April 2019, Northern No. 142036 was stood with the 13.20 service to Lancaster. The train was making a connection with the 14.15 sailing to Douglas.

Merseyrail-liveried First North Western Class 142 No. 142058 was departing from Heysham Port with the 12.58 to Morecambe on 27 October 2001. The single line to the terminus at Heysham, alongside the Isle of Man ferry berth, is the last remnant of the once extensive former Midland Railway westerly outpost here. The only rail freight here are the flask trains to the nuclear power station via the single-track link visible on the left.

Northern Class 144 No. 144011 was stood at Bare Lane awaiting departure with the 74-mile 12.32 Morecambe to Leeds service on 1 October 2018. The Morecambe branch services gain access to the WCML at Morecambe South Junction, located 1.93 miles north of Lancaster station.

A view of the last operational industrial aerial ropeway in the UK, and its bridge across the A683, at Claughton Manor brickworks on 18 April 2022. The ropeway connects the Hanson brickworks to a shale quarry on Claughton Moor and is supported by twenty-six gantries over its 1.25-mile length. The system climbs to 750 feet and is gravity operated. At any one time there are forty to forty-five buckets in operation, and a round trip takes approximately thirty-two minutes.

Having travelled 120 miles along the Cumbrian coast and joining the WCML at Carnforth, DRS Class 37/4 No. 37558 *Avro Vulcan XH558* was almost at journey's end. It is passing over St George's Quay on the approach to Lancaster while providing the power at the rear of the 11.56 departure from Carlisle on 24 February 2018.

Virgin Trains Class 390 Pendolino No. 390124 was running along platform 4 as it arrived at Lancaster with the 14.40 Glasgow Central to London Euston service on 20 August 2019.

Running northbound on the Down through line, DRS Class 88 No. 88005 *Minerva* was winding its way through Lancaster with the 12.16 Daventry to Mossend intermodal service on 20 August 2019.

In BR Intercity Swallow livery, HST power car No. 43159 was departing from Lancaster at the rear of the 09.10 Aberdeen to Plymouth service on 25 August 1997. Almost ten years previously, No. 43159 (with No. 43102) set the world speed record for diesel traction while running on the East Coast Main Line between Thirsk and Northallerton, the power cars reaching 148.5 mph on 1 November 1987 – a record that remains unbroken.

Rekindling the sight and sound of pre-electrification days when pairs of Class 50s roamed along the northern section of the WCML, No. 50007 *Hercules* and No. 50049 *Defiance* were passing Forton with the return leg of the Cumbrian Hoovers tour from Carlisle to Birmingham International on 14 April 2018. Prominent on the skyline is the restaurant tower on the northbound carriageway of the M6 motorway at the Lancaster south services, built in 1965.

Class 90 Nos 90045 and 90047, in contrasting Freightliner liveries, were passing New Lane at Brock with the 11.52 Daventry to Coatbridge intermodal service on 6 April 2019. Hidden behind the trees is the M6, which parallels the WCML for several miles between Preston and Lancaster.

Pendolino No. 390124 was hurrying southbound through the site of Barton and Broughton station with the 12.43 Carlisle to London Euston Avanti West Coast service on 24 April 2021. The vintage Ferguson TE tractor was stood on the cobbled approach roadway to the former station building. Barton and Broughton station was closed by the LMS in 1939.

DB Cargo Class 66 No. 66070 was stood in the Down loop at Barton and Broughton with the 11.18 Daventry to Grangemouth intermodal on 24 April 2021.

Transpennine Express Nova 1 Class 802 No. 802204 was passing over Fylde Road Viaduct on the northern approach to Preston with the 06.58 Craigentinny Depot to Preston crew training run on 13 November 2021. The stone arch below the rear of the leading car once took the now drained Lancaster Canal underneath the WCML.

The original 1840 stone bridge of the Lancaster & Preston Junction Railway was feeling the strain as the 84-ton Class 90 No. 90026 passed over Fylde Road on the northern exit from Preston with the 07.06 Euston to Carlisle 'The Lakelander' on 1 June 2013. To enable modern traffic to pass under the bridge, the roadway beneath has been lowered.

Rolling back the years, LSL Class 87 No. 87002 *Royal Sovereign*, with its rake of matching Mk 3 stock, was passing Fylde Junction at Preston with the 07.10 London Euston to Glasgow Central 'The Electric Scot' on 26 January 2022.

With the 309-foot spire of St Walburge's Church on the skyline, Class 25 Nos 25106 and 25120 were about to pass over Maudland Junction with PCA cement wagons on the approach to Preston on 15 May 1982. The former Longridge branch line diverged from the WCML in the right foreground. In the left background is the Preston PSB with a Class 108 DMU stabled in Croft Street sidings.

With empty PCA cement wagons and HEA coal hoppers in the consist, Class 20 Nos 20042 and 20209 were passing through the site of Deepdale station as they returned from the coal concentration depot at nearby Fletcher Road on 16 May 1986. The station at Deepdale closed in May 1930 with the cessation of passenger services along the 7-mile Preston to Longridge branch.

At a location that has now disappeared beneath new development, this is the mile-long private single-track branch from the former Preston to Longridge line at Ribbleton. It served the Courtaulds Rayon factory that had opened in 1938 and is seen with resident Sentinel diesel (10280/1968) on the last day of railway operations, 12 February 1980.

Flanked by Class 47s on both sides, HST power car Nos 43071 and 43097 were accelerating away from platform 3 at Preston with the 07.26 Penzance to Glasgow Central service on 7 September 1991.

With loaded ballast hoppers, Class 31 No. 31188 was approaching Kirkham North Junction en route to the Blackpool South branch on 8 March 1997. The 11-mile coast line between Kirkham and Blackpool South had a month-long engineering possession in place when all the track and ballast was renewed from end to end.

With the greens of the Royal Lytham and St Annes Golf Club as a backdrop, No. 142052 is seen in its original BR Provincial Services blue livery. It was departing from the former lengthy island platform at Ansdell and Fairhaven with the 16.15 Preston to Blackpool South service on 15 September 1988. The former double-track coast line from Kirkham had been singled in 1986.

With the traffic waiting at the barriers, the tail end of No. 142044 was passing over the B5259 while departing from the rural Moss Side station with the 13.49 Blackpool South to Preston service on 29 December 2018. No. 142044 was amongst the first batch of Northern 142s, which were officially withdrawn from service on 12 August 2019.

Following singling of the route, much disused infrastructure was still in place at the stations between Kirkham and Blackpool South in the late 1980s. An almost new No. 142067 was passing under the disused footbridge as it departed from Lytham with an Ormskirk to Blackpool South service on 15 August 1988.

The motive power at the 10.25-inch-gauge Lytham St Annes Miniature Railway on 17 July 2022. *St Annes Express* is a BR Western diesel look-alike that had been built by Severn-Lamb of Stratford-upon-Avon (7321/1973). In the background is *Harry's Dream*, a 2-6-0 steam outline diesel built in 2005. The railway runs in a 700-yard loop on the seafront and opened in 1973.

With its Manchester–Blackpool white stripe, a three-car BRCW Class 104 DMU formed of cars M50526, M59182 and M50474 was stood at Lytham St Annes with a Blackpool South to Kirkham service on 19 September 1979. Following the singling of the line in 1986, the station seen here was demolished, its replacement having a single platform and basic facilities.

Northern (ex-East Midlands Railway) Class 156 No. 156415 was running alongside Raleigh Avenue as it departed from Squires Gate with the 08.56 Preston to Blackpool South service on 28 May 2022. The skyline is dominated by the 235-foot-high Big One rollercoaster at Blackpool Pleasure Beach.

With the traditional wooden rollercoasters of the Pleasure Beach as a backdrop, No. 142027, in unbranded Greater Manchester livery, was departing from Blackpool Pleasure Beach on the last leg of its journey with the 09.25 Colne to Blackpool South First North Western service on 19 February 2000. The distant board is for the terminus and end of the line at nearby Blackpool South, located just 0.5 miles away.

In refurbished livery, a Class 108 two-car DMU formed of cars M50974 and M56257 was stood at Blackpool South on 9 July 1979. To the right is the track bed of the Marton Direct Line, which once allowed trains to run from Kirkham without taking the circuitous coastal route. There were once multiple running lines through Waterloo Road bridge, along with carriage sidings and a complex array of trackwork leading to the seafront terminus at Blackpool Central, which closed in November 1964.

In the final week of the old-style Blackpool Tramway before it was closed for upgrade/ modernisation, Centenary Cars 644 and 645 were passing at Madison Avenue, Bispham, on 30 October 2011. Eight Centenary Cars were built between 1985 and 1988 (Nos 641–648), with the bodies being made by East Lancashire Coachbuilders at Blackburn. They were the last first-generation trams to be built for a UK tramway.

With the A585 Kirkham Bypass under construction, Class 47/4 No. 47517 *Andrew Carnegie* was passing Kirkham North Junction with the 12.50 Blackpool North to London Euston service on 14 July 1990. A BR 22-ton tube wagon in departmental use was stood in the District Civil Engineers sidings.

Class 37/4 No. 37426 was passing through Kirkham North Junction with the seven-coach 17.14 Manchester Victoria to Blackpool North service on 17 August 1991. The coast line to and from Blackpool South is on the right of this scene.

Class 40 No. 40079 was passing through Poulton-le-Fylde with a Blackpool North to Newcastle Saturday-only working on 28 June 1980. This was the period when there were numerous dated holiday trains running on summer Saturdays to and from Blackpool.

A storm brewing in the distance, Transpennine Express Class 185 No. 185146 was stood at Poulton-le-Fylde with the 12.29 Manchester Airport to Blackpool North service on 23 July 2017. The arm had been removed from the bracket signal in the foreground, which formerly controlled movements onto the disconnected branch to Burn Naze, near Fleetwood.

With the disconnected Fleetwood branch being reclaimed by nature, Northern Class 156 No. 156491 was approaching Poulton-le-Fylde with the 13.21 Blackpool North to Preston service on 23 July 2017. The Poulton and Wyre Railway Society have plans to revive passenger services from Poulton to Thornton-Cleveleys and Burn Naze on the former Fleetwood line.

Following servicing in the carriage sidings at Enfield Road, HST power car No. 43082 was entering Blackpool North ECS with the second stage of the Herfordshire Railtours Settle and Carlisle Circular 125 tour on 8 April 1989.

With the illuminated 518-foot Blackpool Tower lighting up the night sky, Class 37/4 No. 37415 was awaiting departure from Blackpool North with the 19.00 to Liverpool Lime Street on 30 October 1991.

Blackpool Transport English Electric 'Balloon' No. 701 was stood on the siding at Fleetwood Ferry on the Northern end of the 11-mile Blackpool Tramway on 11 April 2015 while on private hire duty. No. 701 was one of twenty-seven double-deck 'Balloons' introduced in 1934/35.

Following a heavy rain shower, a two-car Class 108 DMU formed of cars M54214 and M53927 was stood at the north end of platform 5 at Preston on 30 June 1990. The DMU had arrived from Barrow-in-Furness and was working the short-distance ECS to the sidings at Croft Street, adjacent to Preston PSB.

On a damp 10 February 2018, DRS Class 57/3 No. 57304 *Pride of Cheshire* was running alongside Portway at Preston while working the 05.27 Eastleigh to Preston Docks Pathfinder Tour, 'The Blue Boys Ribble Rouser'. The train was heading towards the headquarters of the Ribble Steam Railway. DRS Class 66 No. 66428 was at the rear.

Having been uncoupled from the 02.55 Lindsey Oil Refinery to Preston Docks bitumen, consisting of fourteen bogie tank wagons and weighing in at 1,760 tonnes, Colas Rail Class 70 No. 70807 was preparing to run round in the exchange sidings at Navigation Way on 17 June 2020. Ribble Rail Sentinel diesel *Progress* (10283/1968) was awaiting to work the loaded wagons to the tar plant at the western end of the former dock estate.

On 11 June 2020, Ribble Rail Sentinel diesel *Progress* (10283/1968), with loaded bitumen tanks, was crossing the swing bridge that takes rail and road over the entrance to the dock basin at Preston. The outer basin is visible beyond the bridge. The lock gates at the Bullnose in the distance give access to the tidal River Ribble. Preston Docks was opened in 1892 and closed in 1981. The line here is also used by the heritage Ribble Steam Railway.

Having departed from Preston, Avanti West Coast 'Pride' Pendolino No. 390119 was getting into its stride as it approached Skew Bridge at Penwortham while working the 07.37 Glasgow Central to London Euston service on 16 April 2021.

Complete with headboard, Class 31/4 No. 31412, in BR Engineers Grey livery, was passing Lostock Hall Junction with the 09.05 Preston to Carlisle Dalesrail service on 2 September 1989. Formed of six coaches, this was a brief period when some of these Sunday out-and-back workings over the Settle & Carlisle via Blackburn were loco-hauled due to a shortage of DMU sets.

In large logo livery, Class 47/4 No. 47485 was passing through Bamber Bridge with the daily Warrington Arpley Yard to Blackburn trip working on 23 July 1990. Bamber Bridge has a busy level crossing located on what was once the A6 trunk road.

With Waterfall Mills as a backdrop, Northern Class 142 No. 142093 was passing over Albert Street as it departed from Mill Hill with the 10.57 Preston to Colne service on 14 December 2018. Waterfall Mills was originally owned by John Fish Ltd and dated from 1851/52. The mill was extended between 1858 and 1860 and had a further extension in 1879.

With Colas Rail Class 56 Nos 56090 and 56094 stood in Taylor Street loop on the west side of Blackburn with the 10.05 Preston Docks to Lindsey bitumen empties, No. 142018 was passing over Bolton Junction while working the 09.25 Clitheroe to Rochdale (via Manchester Victoria) on 9 August 2018.

Former BR Class 04 No. D2272 was stood in the British Fuels coal depot at King Street, Blackburn, on 25 April 1982. Built in 1958 at the Robert Stephenson and Hawthorn factory at Darlington, the Class 04 was withdrawn from BR service in October 1970. When the coal yard closed in the 1990s, the Class 04 passed into preservation. The site of the coal yard at Blackburn is now a Northern Rail DMU depot.

GBRf Class 66 No. 66757 *West Somerset Railway* was crossing from the Down East Lancashire to the Up East Lancashire to access the Up and Down goods loop at Blackburn while working the 05.54 Avonmouth to Clitheroe cement empties on 4 November 2021.

Northern Class 142 No. 142089 was stood at Blackburn with the terminated 09.57 Preston to Colne service on 3 December 2019. The station at Blackburn consists of three through platforms and a west-facing bay, having been rebuilt in 2000.

A HST in BR Intercity Swallow livery was passing through the Lancashire & Yorkshire Railway iron and glass train shed at Blackburn on 31 March 1990. Power car No. 43099 was leading the Hertfordshire Railtours Hills of the North tour from London St Pancras to Carlisle. The station at Blackburn dated from 1888 and was totally rebuilt at platform level in 2000.

Just east of Blackburn, Class 66 No. 66093 was taking the Ribble Valley route at Daisyfield Junction with the 05.00 Avonmouth to Clitheroe Castle cement formed of empty JPA wagons on 22 July 2017.

With the houses on Whalley New Road as a background, GBRf Class 66 No. 66756 *Royal Corps of Signals* was passing Brownhill on the north-east side of Blackburn with the 05.00 Avonmouth to Clitheroe cement empties on 22 January 2022.

Northern three-car Class 150/0 No. 150001 was dropping down the bank from Ramsgreave and Wilpshire while working the 15.25 Clitheroe to Rochdale service on 22 July 2021. No. 150001 was one of a pair of three-car prototype Class 150/0 units built at BREL York in 1984 (150001/150002).

Colas Rail Class 37 No. 37421 was leading the 14.13 Blackpool North to Derby RTC Network Rail track inspection service crossing Whalley Viaduct on 23 April 2021. Whalley Viaduct consists of forty-eight brick arches, utilising over 7 million bricks, and was constructed for the Bolton, Blackburn, Clitheroe & West Yorkshire Railway between 1846 and 1850. It is the largest viaduct in Lancashire.

Northern Class 153 No. 153316 and Class 150 No. 150147 were awaiting departure from Clitheroe on 17 July 2017. Located 10 miles from Blackburn, Clitheroe station is the terminating point for Ribble Valley Line passenger services. The original station closed in 1962, and when passenger services restarted in 1994 a new platform was constructed adjacent to the former station building, which has become an art gallery.

GBRf Class 66 No. 66779 *Evening Star* was reversing away from the Ribble Valley route along the cement works branch at Horrocksford Junction. It is with the 09.34 Carlisle Yard to Clitheroe cement empties, which is formed of JPA bogie wagons, on 5 May 2021.

Ex-BR Clayton Type 1 Class 17 No. 8 (former D8568) was stabled with some BR Presflo cement wagons at the Ribble cement works at Clitheroe on 3 May 1982. There were 117 of these locos built. No. D8568 had been new in 1964 but was withdrawn from BR service in 1971. Fortunately, this unique locomotive has since passed into preservation.

GBRf Class 66 No. 66710 was stood in the Castle Cement works at Clitheroe with empty JPA bogie wagons on 25 June 2018. The industrial diesel shunter visible on the right is one of a resident pair at the works, built at Vulcan Foundry in 1975 (Works No. GECT 5396). The loco originally worked at BSC Shotton before coming to Clitheroe in the 1980s.

A two-car BRCW Class 104 DMU formed of cars M53468 and M53494 was departing from Rishton with a Preston to Colne service on 6 October 1984. Rishton is a small town on the A678 Blackburn to Burnley road, and is midway between Blackburn and Accrington.

West Coast Class 47 No. 47772 *Carnforth TMD* was passing over Accrington Viaduct, bringing up the rear of the Sheffield to Blackburn leg of the Pennine Limited on a cold 3 March 2018.

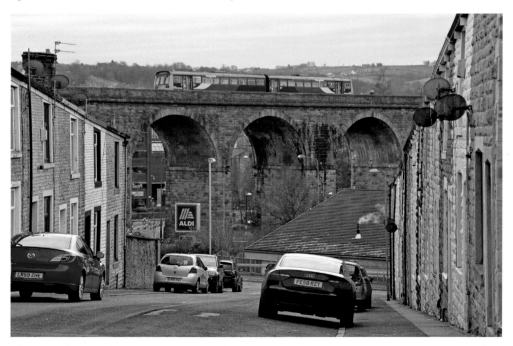

The view along Malt Street as Northern Class 142 No. 142049 was crossing Accrington Viaduct while working the 11.11 Colne to Preston service on 18 January 2019. The Grade II listed Accrington Viaduct was built by the East Lancashire Railway in 1847. It consisted of nineteen stone arches and was 60 feet tall.

With the Pennines as a backdrop, Northern Class 142 No. 142052 was passing over Bank Top Viaduct as it departed from Burnley Central with the 11.11 Colne to Preston service on 15 November 2018. Completed in 1848, Bank Top (Ashfield) Viaduct consists of fourteen stone arches.

Passengers were greeting No. 142052 at Nelson with the 12.11 Colne to Preston service on 9 November 2018. Of the East Lancashire line stations, Nelson has retained its former Lancashire & Yorkshire Railway iron and glass platform canopy. The route here has been single track since 1986.

With Pendle Hill in the background, the tail end of No. 142038 was passing over Barkerhouse Road/Chaffers siding level crossing at Nelson while working the final leg of the 11.57 Preston to Colne service on 21 May 2019.

Former West Midlands Class 150/1 No. 150115 was bringing some colour to a wintery scene as it departed from the terminus at Colne with the 15.35 service to Preston on 5 February 2012. No. 150115 was one of eighteen 150s transferred from Tyseley depot at Birmingham to Newton Heath in 2011.

Northern Class 156/150 Nos 156460 and 150224 were stood at Burnley Manchester Road with the 12.28 Accrington to Manchester Victoria service on 13 November 2016. The original station here closed in 1961 but was reopened in 1986, then rebuilt in 2014. This coincided with the opening of the Todmorden Curve, enabling trains to access the Calder Valley route to and from Manchester.

With Dean Farm as a backdrop, DRS Class 37/6 No. 37612 was heading downgrade from Copy Pit summit with a Wigan to Derby RTC Network Rail working on 4 January 2015. Although running through Lancashire, the train was about to cross into West Yorkshire and join the Manchester to Leeds Calder Valley route at Hall Royd Junction, just to the east of Todmorden.

GBRf Class 60 No. 60047 *Faithful* was heading westwards over Gauxholme Viaduct while running between Todmorden and Walsden on the Calder Valley route with the 09.54 Drax Power Station to Liverpool Bulk Terminal biomass empties on 6 April 2022.

Running through the landscape of the Calder Valley, GBRf Class 66 No. 66796 *The Green Progressor*, in its 'HS2 – Cleaner by Rail' livery, was passing over Gauxholme Viaduct with the 08.07 Liverpool Bulk Terminal to Drax Power Station biomass on 6 April 2022. The railway here is flanked by the A646 road and the Rochdale Canal.

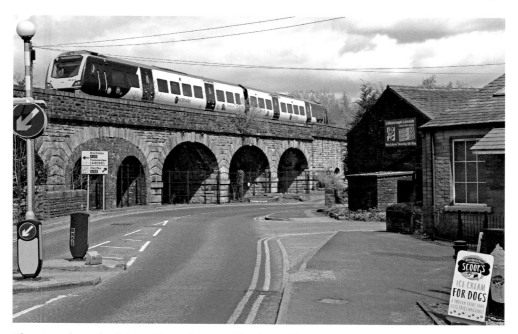

The view along the B6225 Canal Street as Northern Class 195/0 No. 195013 was passing over Littleborough Viaduct with the 12.12 Leeds to Manchester Victoria service on 26 April 2022. The short viaduct with its stone arch over the A58 was designed by George Stephenson for the Manchester & Leeds Railway and was completed in 1839.

In de-branded EWS livery, DB Cargo Class 66 No. 66095 was passing Clegg Hall on the eastern approach to Rochdale with the 05.40 Wilton to Knowsley empty binliner on 19 January 2022.

Northern Class 142 Nos 142043 and 142065 were awaiting departure from Rochdale with the 12.16 Manchester Victoria to Leeds service on 23 August 2016.

In Merseyrail livery, First North Western Class 142 No. 42045 was stood at Shaw and Crompton on the Oldham Loop with the 15.45 service to Wigan Wallgate on 3 October 2002. Shaw and Crompton station closed along with the rest of the Oldham Loop, from Rochdale to Thorpes Bridge Junction at Newton Heath, on 3 October 2009 in readiness for conversion to the Metrolink system.

The view along Winterbottom Street as Metrolink M5000 No. 3091 was departing from Westwood with a Shaw via Oldham service on 2 March 2022. On the skyline towards the rear of No. 3091 is the former Anchor cotton spinning mill, which dates from 1881. This section of the Metrolink is part of the section that takes the tramway through Oldham town centre. It opened in 2014.

Northern Class 155 No. 155346 was passing Castleton with the 12.08 Manchester Victoria to Leeds service on 15 May 2011. Beyond the signal box is the connection to the heritage East Lancashire Railway at Heywood.

Totally unnoticed, ex-LNER A3 No. 60103 *Flying Scotsman* was passing over Oldham Road while running through Mills Hill with the 07.35 York NRM to Castleton working on 21 August 2018. The loco and support coach were en route to the East Lancashire Railway for the Scotsman in Steam event.

Class 08 No. 08721 *Longsight TMD* brings up the rear of the 11.25 Heywood to Bury running between Heywood Street and Market Street on the East Lancashire Railway at Bury on 17 April 2016. In the past this location had multiple running lines and sidings, in the days when this was an east–west strategic link from Bolton through Bury to Castleton on the Calder Valley route; in effect, it was a Manchester railway bypass.

A two-car Class 504 EMU, with Driving Motor Brake Second M65452 leading, was arriving at Bury Interchange with a service from Manchester Victoria on 27 April 1991. The Manchester–Bury 1,200 VDC electric line became part of the Manchester Metrolink system in 1992.

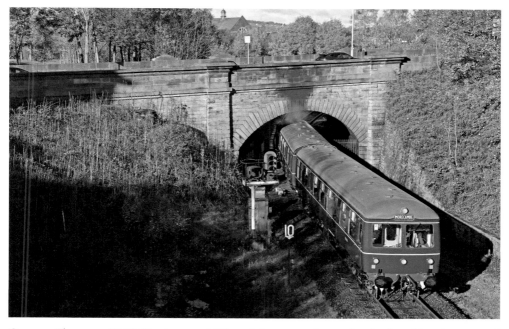

Cravens Class 105 DMU (E56171 and SC51485) was passing under the A56 Manchester road on the exit from Bury with the 09.45 Rawtenstall to Heywood East Lancashire Railway service on 5 November 2017. The stone arch is the original ELR structure, dating from 1848. There was another alongside on the left, now backfilled, that once took a pair of tracks westbound to Bolton. The Bury to Bolton route was closed in 1970.

In 2006 the East Lancashire Railway imported a Northern Ireland Railways Class 80 DEMU driving car No. 8099 for use as a source of engine spares for their ex-BR Southern Region Class 207 unit. The car was stood on an isolated section of 5-foot-3-inch-gauge track at Bury Castlecroft Yard on 3 September 2006.

Carrying the fictious 'Great Midlands Trains' livery, ex-Northern Class 144 No. 144009 was departing ECS from Ramsbottom during the autumn diesel gala at the East Lancashire Railway on 17 September 2021. The Class 144 had worked the 16.45 Bury to Ramsbottom service.

BR Standard 2-6-4T No. 80080 was arriving at Rawtenstall with the 14.40 service from Bury on 10 March 2019. The heritage East Lancashire Railway opened in three stages: Bury to Ramsbottom in 1987, Ramsbottom to Rawtenstall in 1991 and Bury to Heywood in 2003, giving an end-to-end distance of 12 miles.

1,200 VDC Class 504 Driving Trailer Second M77181 was arriving at Prestwich with a Bury Interchange to Manchester Victoria service on 3 September 1989. There were twenty-six two-car Class 504 EMUs built at Wolverton Works in 1959. They had a unique side contact current collection from the live rails.

The Leyland Motors sidings alongside the WCML at Farington on 1 May 1982. The works diesel shunter was John Fowler 0-4-0 (JF4210108/1955). The BR Mk 1 brake coach (M21234) was awaiting transfer to the Leyland National bus plant at Workington to receive an experimental Leyland National body, being renumbered to ADB977091. The Leyland Motors empire that made buses and lorries has now gone, and the sidings here were refurbished for use by Northern DMUs during electrification work at Blackpool North in 2018.

In Engineers Grey livery, Class 31/4 No. 31466 was departing from Leyland on the Down fast with the 17.02 Liverpool Lime Street to Preston service on 23 May 1990. The guard is looking back from a Scotrail-branded Mk 1 BSK, while the rest of the train was made up of Network South East-livered stock.

In branded London Northwestern livery, Class 350/4 No. 350403 was passing Buckshaw Parkway while working the 13.10 Manchester Airport to Glasgow Central Transpennine Express service on 19 January 2020. Buckshaw Parkway serves Buckshaw Village and is built on the site of the Euxton Royal Ordnance Factory, which opened in 1938 and closed in 2007. The station was opened in October 2011 on what has been described as one of the largest brownfield development sites in Europe.

Ex-LMS Stanier Pacific No. 46233 *Duchess of Sutherland* was cantering through Chorley with the Cumbrian Mountain Express 06.04 Crewe to Carlisle on 5 August 2017.

Class 47/4 No. 47423 was passing Chorley with a Glasgow Central to Manchester Victoria service on 29 December 1988. To the left of this scene there is now a dual carriageway (the A6) and a bus station/interchange. In the foreground is the former goods yard area, which now forms part of the station car park but was then derelict land.

Northern Class 331/0 No. 331010 was arriving at the small station at Adlington with the 14.03 Hazel Grove to Blackpool North service on 25 April 2020. Electric services between Preston and Manchester via Bolton commenced in February 2019.

Class 40 No. 40107 and Class 83 No. 83007 were two of the exhibits at the Horwich Works open day on 16 August 1980. The works was opened by the Lancashire & Yorkshire Railway in 1886 and closed in 1983.

In Greater Manchester PTE livery, Class 142 No. 142006 was departing from Darwen with a Blackburn to Manchester Victoria service on 14 January 1989. Darwen was one of the Lancashire cotton towns but was also home to paint and wallpaper manufacturers.

Dropping downgrade from Bromley Cross towards Bolton, Colas Rail Class 70 No. 70817 was about to pass over the A58 Compton Way while passing Hall i' th' Wood with the diverted 12.10 Carlisle Yard to Chirk Kronospan logs on 5 April 2021.

Ex-First Great Western Class 150/1 No. 150123 and Northern-liveried No. 150142 were heading away from Bolton at Plevna Street while working the 11.45 Manchester Victoria to Clitheroe service on 20 May 2018.

A pair of Newton Heath Cravens Class 105 Power-Twin DMUs were forming a Manchester Victoria to Kirkby service (complete with their nose-to-nose first-class saloons) awaiting departure from Bolton on 23 June 1979. At the rear was Driving Motor Brake Second M50771. The distinctive Cravens Power-Twin fleet were a familiar sight around Lancashire in the 1970s.

Transpennine Express Class 350/4 No. 350410 was passing through Bolton while working the diverted 13.48 Preston to Manchester Airport service on 4 May 2019. TPE had ten of these four-car Siemens-built EMUs in service from 2014 until the fleet was transferred to LNWR in 2019/20.

DRS Class 47/8 No. 47853 *Express* was arriving at Bolton with the 11.37 Manchester Victoria to Preston 'Christmas Shoppex' on 6 December 2014. These services formed additional capacity on the busy Preston to Manchester corridor on pre-Christmas Saturdays.

Virgin Trains 'Thunderbird' Class 57/3 No. 57303 *Alan Tracy* was plodding through Bolton with a diverted Preston to London Euston service on 15 November 2003. This view has been radically altered with the electrification that was completed in 2019. The redundant platform face to the left of this view, where the cars are parked, has been reinstated and now forms platform 5.

With electrification work in progress Northern Class 150 Nos 150103 and 150203 were passing through the deserted platforms at Clifton with the 10.05 Southport to Chester service on 8 April 2018. Just two trains a day (Monday to Saturday) call at Clifton, at what was once a busy junction station. Until 1966 there were additional platforms here for services to Accrington via Bury.

At the disused Kearsley Power Station, former BR Class 05 diesel shunters Nos D2587 and D2595 were stabled on 13 May 1982. The locos had been used at Chadderton Power Station near Oldham, but following closure they were moved into safe storage with other North West CEGB redundant locomotives. Both locos were eventually preserved. Unfortunately the 500 VDC internal overhead electric system at Kearsley has now gone, along with the power station. Housing now covers the entire location.

On the last day of operation at Agecroft on 12 September 1981, RSH 0-4-0ST *Agecroft No.3* was coupled to BR 20-ton brake van B955208, giving rides up and down the four long sidings that ran parallel to the Manchester–Bolton line and were in the shadow of the cooling towers of the adjacent power station. Operated by a trio of identical Robert Stephenson and Hawthorns 0-4-0 saddle tanks – *Agecroft 1, 2* and *3* – the system was made redundant when a conveyor was installed between Agecroft Colliery and the power station.

Transpennine Express Class 185 No. 185103 was passing through the industrial landscape of Pendleton as it was running towards Salford with the 10.23 Barrow-in-Furness to Manchester Airport service on 8 April 2018. The former Kingston Mill dominates the immediate background. To the left of the Class 185 is the site of the Manchester, Bolton and Bury Canal. The railway and canal once ran parallel from Agecroft to Salford. The canal was closed entirely in 1961.

With the ever-changing cityscape behind, DB Cargo Class 66 No. 66102 was running through Salford Central with the 07.20 Wilton to Knowsley empty binliner on 20 April 2018.

On what was once a four track section of railway, DB Cargo Class 66 No. 66100 *Armistice 100 1918–2018* was passing through Daisy Hill station with the 07.25 Wilton to Knowsley empty binliner on 6 May 2020. This service is now the only non-passenger train over the route from Salford Crescent to Wigan Wallgate.

Passengers step forward as Class 150/2 No. 150273 arrives at Hindley while working the 12.14 Manchester Victoria to Kirkby service on 28 May 2016. The station once had four tracks. Platform 2, formerly an island platform, is now the site of a well-maintained garden complete a Northern Rail-liveried windmill. The gardens here are maintained by the Friends of Hindley Station.

With the driver looking back, Class 87 No. 87023 *Velocity* – still carrying its (worn) BR Intercity livery – was stood at Wigan North Western with the 13.03 London Euston to Lancaster Virgin Trains service on 18 June 2000. Wigan North Western was totally rebuilt prior to electrification of the WCML in 1973.

With plenty of insect debris on its cab front, Class 86/2 No. 86242 *James Kennedy GC* was arriving at Wigan North Western with the Sunday Virgin Trains Cross Country 07.15 Penzance to Edinburgh 'Cornish Scot' on 17 May 1998.

With the WCML in the background and the route to Southport in the foreground, Derby Class 108 DMU sets were Sunday resting in the Up sidings adjacent to Wigan Wallgate Junction on 2 November 1986.

DB Cargo Class 66 No. 66142 was approaching Wigan Wallgate with the 10.50 Knowsley to Wilton binliner, while overhead a Virgin Pendolino was departing from Wigan North Western with the 08.43 London Euston to Edinburgh service on 20 April 2018.

A contrast of liveries at Wigan Wallgate, with former London Midland Class 150/1 No. 150109 in the bay awaiting departure with the 16.58 to Kirkby. Northern Class 156 No. 156488 was arriving with the 16.24 Southport to Leeds service on 22 June 2019. The former L&YR station at Wigan has two through platforms and a west-facing bay.

The Central Wagon Works scrapyard at Ince, near Wigan, scrapped many redundant BR steam locomotives in the 1960s. On 28 July 1982 the yard was scrapping obsolete BR wagons. The yard shunter was this Ruston and Hornsby 48DS Diesel (349032/1953). It had been lifted off the track and, like many scrapyard shunters when they have served their useful purpose, scrapping awaits. The Coles crane in the background, with its electromagnet, was doing all the work in the yard.

Class 25 No. 25080 was stood with the breakdown/re-railing train at Wigan Springs Branch TMD on 12 August 1984. The loco was built at Darlington Works as No. D5230 in October 1963. It was renumbered to 25080 in January 1973 and was withdrawn from service in September 1985. MC Metals at Springburn consigned No. 25080 to history in May 1993.

Having left the WCML at Haydock Branch Junction, GBRf Class 60 No. 60026 *Helvellyn* was running along the remnant of the Great Central Railway's Lowton St Marys to St Helens route, arriving at Ashton-in-Makerfield with the 09.10 from Tuebrook Sidings with sand for the manufacture of concrete on 9 March 2022. The train would access the Edge Green terminal via the spur on the left. The line closed as a through route in 1952.

Avanti West Coast Pendolino No. 390129 was hurrying through Golborne with the 12.40 Glasgow Central to London Euston service on 5 April 2022. The derelict former goods shed, complete with a section of track still in situ, was closed in 1967. Golborne station closed in 1961.

The preserved main line registered Class 86/2 No. 86259/E3137 *Peter Pan/Les Ross* had just passed through Winwick Junction with the 07.10 London Euston to Carlisle Cumbrian Coast Express on 9 April 2016.

At the rear of what was once the locomotive-erecting shop at Vulcan Foundry, a Ruston and Hornsby 165 0-6-0 diesel (310088/1951) was in the yard on 28 July 1982. The works was then owned by Ruston Diesels, and the loco (which had been built in the Lincoln factory of R&H) had been brought to Newton-le-Willows for apprentice training. Vulcan Foundry closed in 2002 and the site is now covered with a housing development.

On the historic original Liverpool to Manchester route, which was electrified in 2015, Class 319 No. 319366, in Northern Electrics livery, was stood at Newton-le-Willows with the 09.16 Liverpool Lime Street to Manchester Airport service on 27 May 2016.

Class 142 No. 142041 was approaching Midge Hall with the 11.40 Preston to Ormskirk service on 13 September 1986. The Class 142 was passing through the disused platforms of Midge Hall station, which had been closed in October 1961, on what was once the double-track main line between Preston and Liverpool Exchange. The line from Farington Curve Junction to Midge Hall retained double track until August 1983.

A two-car Class 108 DMU, formed of cars M51565 and M53925, was departing the village of Croston with a Preston to Ormskirk service on 27 July 1985. The unit was passing the remains of the loading gauge at what was once the entrance to the goods yard.

The doyen Class 153 single unit No. 153301 was crossing the River Douglas on the approach to Rufford while working the 10.07 Preston to Ormskirk service on 19 November 2011.

A two-car Class 116 Suburban DMU formed of cars M53870 and M53923 was arriving at Rufford with a Preston to Ormskirk service on 12 April 1988. When the Preston to Ormskirk line was singled in 1970, double track forming a passing loop was retained at Rufford.

Plenty of custom on a bank holiday Monday, as Nos 142067 and 150119 were stood at Burscough Bridge with the 11.03 Manchester Airport to Southport service on 7 May 2018. There were once connecting north and south curves at Burscough that linked the Wigan–Southport route to the Preston–Ormskirk line.

With the locks on the Leeds and Liverpool Canal in the foreground, Northern Class 142 No. 142062 was running between Hoscar and Burscough with a Wigan to Southport empty stock working on 1 December 2012.

In rural west Lancashire, the Windmill Animal Farm at Burscough has a 15-inch-gauge miniature railway with an out-and-back distance of 0.75 miles. At the main station on 26 April 2015 was a diesel that once worked at the now closed line at Dudley Zoo; it had been built by G&S Light Engineering of Stourbridge in 1957.

Running on diesel power, Northern Class 769 'Flex' No. 769458 was arriving at the village of Parbold with the 12.51 Alderley Edge to Southport service on 2 April 2022.

Northern Class 150/1 Nos 150145 and 150117 were arriving at Appley Bridge with the 15.23 Southport to Manchester Airport service on 4 June 2016.

DB Cargo Class 66 No. 66142 was passing under the substantial stone bridge that takes Church Street over the railway while running eastbound through Orrell with the 10.50 Knowsley to Wilton containerised refuse service on 6 April 2018. This section of railway was once part of the Lancashire & Yorkshire Railway's Manchester Victoria to Liverpool (Exchange) main line.

Passengers were greeting No. 150139's arrival at Rainford with the 12.14 Manchester Victoria to Kirkby on 13 February 2016. Rainford was once a junction station for the now closed routes to Ormskirk and St Helens. West of Rainford, the former double-track route towards Liverpool is single track and now terminates at Headbolt Lane.

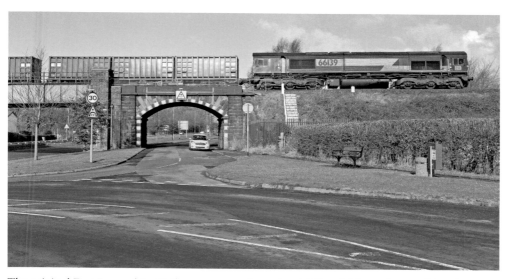

The original East Lancashire Railway stone arch on the old Ormskirk road was taking the strain as No. 66139 was passing Rainford with the 10.50 Knowsley to Wilton binliner service on 9 February 2018.

In de-branded London Midland livery, No. 150109 was approaching the stop block at Kirkby, at the conclusion of its 12-mile journey with the 14.58 departure from Wigan Wallgate on 22 June 2019. In 2023, Kirkby became a through station once more, with Merseyrail services extended eastwards to a new station at Headbolt Lane.

Merseyrail Class 507 No. 507005 was stood in the single-track terminus at Kirkby with the 14.43 departure to Liverpool Central on 22 June 2019. The diesel service to Wigan terminates at the other side of the bridge at the rear of the Class 507. When Merseyrail services were extended to the east of Kirkby in 2023, the interchange between electric and diesel services was moved to Headbolt Lane station.

A three-car ex-LMS Class 502 formed of cars M28354M, M29581M and M29863M was awaiting departure from the market town of Ormskirk with a service to Liverpool Central on 16 September 1978. Built at Derby, the Class 502s were introduced between 1939 and 1941, and lasted in service until 1980. Ormskirk station was heavily rationalised when the non-electrified route from Preston was singled in 1970.

With Class 507 No. 507011 on the 15.08 Ormskirk to Liverpool Central Merseyrail Northern Line service, Northern Class 156 No. 156455 was departing from Ormskirk with the 15.01 Ormskirk to Preston on 3 April 2021. The former double-track main line at Ormskirk was split into two separate single-line sections in 1970.

Rejoining double track, Class 507 Nos 507016 and 507003 were departing from Ormskirk to commenceme their 19-mile journey with the 15.07 Ormskirk to Hunts Cross Merseyrail Northern Line service on 31 May 2020.

Opened in 1967, the 2-foot-gauge West Lancashire Light Railway at Hesketh Bank runs around part of a former brickworks in semi-rural surroundings for approximately 430 yards. On 17 May 2015, Ultrilas, an 0-4-0T built by Orenstein and Koppel in 1907, had arrived at Becconsall with a service from Delph.

On a route that was once electrified to Meols Cop and Crossens (on the route to Preston that closed in 1964), ex-East Midlands Railway Class 156 No. 156401 was approaching St Lukes in the Southport suburbs with the 13.36 Southport to Stalybridge Northern service on 5 January 2022.

Class 20 Nos 20010 and 20175 were shunting empty coaches at Southport on 17 September 1989. The local newspaper had organised a series of trips between Southport, Wigan and Manchester using ex-LMS Jubilee 4-6-0 No. 45596 *Bahamas*, and the Class 20s were the stock release locos at Southport. In the foreground were Class 507 Nos 507003 and 507013.

In its distinctive 'The Beatles Story' livery at the Albert Dock, Class 508 No. 508111 was arriving at the terminus at Southport with the 09.56 departure from Hunts Cross on 21 July 2021.

A joint BR/Steamport Museum open day at Southport on 11 September 1982 had a service between Southport station and the former engine shed in Derby Road, operated by Birkenhead-based Class 03 No. 03189 with a Class 108 DMU M52051/M51936 providing the passenger accommodation. With former West Lancashire Railway land in the background, No. 03189 was working one of the shuttles away from the museum. Steamport eventually closed in 1999.

Against a backdrop that has now been totally redeveloped, Regional Railways Class 37/4 No. 37414 *Cathays C&W Works 1846-1993* was reversing its train of five Regional Railways coaches into the loop alongside the old excursion platform at Southport in preparation for running round on 14 August 1994. The Class 37 had arrived with the 17.19 departure from Manchester Victoria.

A quiet moment at the Pleasureland terminus of the Lakeside Miniature Railway (LMR) at Southport on 23 May 2004. The loco was a BR Class 52 Western diesel look-alike, *Princess Anne*, which had been built by Severn-Lamb of Stratford-upon-Avon for the LMR in 1971. The 15-inch-gauge railway is 1,500 yards in length and was opened in May 1911.

Freightliner Class 66/9 No. 66956 was stood at Birkdale station with a rake of Network Rail JNA wagons during engineering work on 9 February 2014. The Up line had been lifted and the wagons were being filled with the old ballast.

Network Rail Windhoff MPV DR98951/DR98901 was passing Dover Road at Birkdale with a Southport to Sandhills de-icing run on 21 March 2015. With a clear night and a frost in the forecast, the conductor rails were being coated with anti-freeze solution.

Late on an August evening in 1978, a Class 502 three-car EMU with Driving Trailer Second M29896M leading was stood at Ainsdale with a Liverpool Central to Southport service. The driving cars of this set, M28361M and M29896M, are now the only surviving members of the class and are being restored by the Class 502 Preservation Trust at the Merseyside Transport Trust premises at Burscough.

Viewed from the sand dunes, a feature of the landscape to the South of Ainsdale, Class 507 No. 507014 was passing the end of Patterdale Close while running at speed between Ainsdale and Freshfield with a Southport to Hunts Cross service on 19 July 2015.

In its original BR blue and grey livery, Class 507 No. 507006 was arriving at Formby with a Southport to Hunts Cross service on 1 September 1991. The semaphore signals were replaced by colour lights in 1994.

Ex-LMS Class 502 Driving Trailer M29889M was at the rear of a Southport to Liverpool Central service at Hall Road on 19 April 1979. The car had been originally a composite containing both first- and second-class saloons. The last of the Class 502s were withdrawn in 1980.

On 18 October 1996, the line up in the sidings at Hall Road Depot at Crosby included No. 507004 in blue/grey livery, two ex-London District Class 501 Sandite/de-icing cars and a trio of ex-Southern Region Class 73 electro-diesels, Nos 73906, 73005 and 73002. Hall Road depot opened in 1939 and closed in 1997.

Class 507 No. 507030 was hurrying northbound through the west Lancashire countryside at Aughton while running between Maghull North and Town Green with the 10.47 Liverpool Central to Ormskirk Northern Line service on 24 April 2022.

The houses in Eskdale Road provide a backdrop to No. 508130 as it departed from Orrell Park with an Ormskirk to Liverpool Central service on 14 March 2015. Orrell Park is located between Aintree and Walton-on-the-Hill, and the small urban station is surrounded by busy streets.

Looking north, Nos 508117 and 507014 were passing through the site of the new Maghull North station with a limited-stop Boxing Day 12.46 Ormskirk to Liverpool Central Northern Line service on 26 December 2017. The station cost £13 million and was opened in June 2018.

West Coast Railways Class 47 Nos 47245 and 47826, with the Branch Line Society's Bootle Brush rail tour, were stood on the coast line at Sandhills Junction awaiting the passage of No. 508138 working the 11.35 Liverpool Central to Kirkby service on 8 December 2019.

In its retro BR Railfreight Construction livery, GBRf Class 66 No. 66793 was emerging from Seaforth Docks with the 11.15 Liverpool Bulk Terminal to Drax Power Station loaded biomass on 30 March 2021.

With Huyton station visible in the distance, Transpennine Express Nova 1 Class 802 No. 802212 had just passed through Roby with the 12.54 Liverpool Lime Street to Newcastle service on 9 February 2022. The historic Liverpool to Manchester route was electrified in 2015.

Northern Class 323 No. 323238 was stood at Rainhill while working the 09.00 Liverpool Lime Street to Warrington Bank Quay service on 25 May 2019. The station name board commemorates the Rainhill Trials of 1829.

Where it all began. 2019 marked the 190th anniversary of the Rainhill Trials (1829). The village of Rainhill organised a celebration to commemorate the event over the spring bank holiday, 25–27 May. The highlight of Rocket 190 was the appearance of the replica *Rocket* from the National Railway Museum. On Saturday 25 May, the locomotive was on display in Exchange Place. This was its first appearance at Rainhill since the Rocket 150 cavalcade and celebrations in May 1980.

Bibliography

Brown, Joe, *Liverpool & Manchester Railway Atlas* (Manchester: Crecy Publishing, 2021)
Bridge, Mike, *Track Atlas of Mainland Britain: 2nd Edition* (Sheffield: Platform 5 Publishing, 2012)
Joy, David, *Railways in Lancashire A Pictorial History* (Clapham: Dalesman Publishing, 1975)
Marshall, John, *Forgotten Railways North West England* (Newton Abbot: David & Charles Publishing, 1981)